THE RIDE OF YOUR LIFE

PROPERTY OF:
Drama Department
City of London
School for Girls
Barbican, London EC2Y 8BB

Mick Gordon

THE RIDE OF YOUR LIFE

(On Evolution)

OBERON BOOKS
LONDON

First published in 2009 by Oberon Books Ltd
521 Caledonian Road, London N7 9RH
Tel: 020 7607 3637 / Fax: 020 7607 3629
e-mail: info@oberonbooks.com
www.oberonbooks.com

The Ride of Your Life copyright © Mick Gordon 2009

Mick Gordon is hereby identified as author of this play in accordance with section 77 of the Copyright, Designs and Patents Act 1988. The author has asserted his moral rights.

All rights whatsoever in this play are strictly reserved and application for performance etc. should be made before commencement of rehearsal to United Agents, 12-26 Lexington Street, London, W1F 0LE. No performance may be given unless a licence has been obtained, and no alterations may be made in the title or the text of the play without the author's prior written consent.

This book is sold subject to the condition that it shall not by way of trade or otherwise be circulated without the publisher's consent in any form of binding or cover or circulated electronically other than that in which it is published and without a similar condition including this condition being imposed on any subsequent purchaser.

A catalogue record for this book is available from the British Library.

ISBN: 978-1-84002-958-1

Cover design and illustration by Satoshi Kitamura

Printed in Great Britain by CPI Antony Rowe, Chippenham.

For Nici

On Evolution

When the English biologist Thomas Henry Huxley first read Charles Darwin's explanation of how evolution works, he remembered thinking: 'How extremely stupid not to have thought of that.' So it is, that extraordinary ideas, after the fact of explanation, seem obvious.

On the Origin of Species by Means of Natural Selection, or the Preservation of Favoured Races in the Struggle for Life, by Charles Robert Darwin, was published on 24 November 1859. It introduced the world to an amazing idea: That all of life on earth arose from a common ancestor through a branching pattern of evolution. And it put forward an explanation of the mechanism of evolution: Natural Selection. With this idea, and this explanation, Charles Darwin did for biology what Galileo had done for the planets.

Evolution is inevitable because nature cannot help but reproduce itself. And because nature, when it reproduces, makes mistakes. Consider this: All of life on earth results from a series of successful reproductive mistakes. Amazing. Natural Selection is the process by which inherited traits, that make it more likely for an organism to survive and successfully reproduce, become established in a species or population over successive generations. As many more individuals of each population are born than can possibly survive, there will be a frequently recurring struggle for existence. Therefore, if any offspring varies, however slightly, in any manner advantageous to itself under the complex pressures of its given environment, then it will have a better chance of surviving. And so it will be naturally selected.

We now know that inheritance is based on tiny particles called genes. All living things – from viruses to human beings – depend on genes as genes hold the information to build and maintain the cells that make up all living things.

One of the most profound contemporary examples of the evolutionary process at work is AIDS. In its brief history, its agent, which is to say, its genes, have changed. And so a patient may be the home of creatures, descended from those that originally infected him, but as different to their ancestors as humans are from apes. And all because nature cannot help but reproduce itself, and when it does, it makes mistakes, and some mistakes help promote survival.

Before Darwin, it was generally accepted that man came from an archetype created by God, and was set apart from animals. Darwin's discovery showed that creation had taken considerably longer than the Biblical seven days and that man was, in fact, a modified, lineal descendant of other animals. As well as launching a revolution in biology, his insight irrevocably shook the human race's conception of where they had come from. It is no exaggeration to say that with the publication of his book, the notion of life as fixed in a divine mould was dead.

But this is not the same as saying that the idea of religion, or the idea of God, was dead. And this is a very important distinction to make in the teaching of evolution. Science relies on proofs, and is based on evidence. Ideas of religion and ideas of God rely on faith and are based on tradition and practice. Adults can make up their own minds about the usefulness and reliability of their own belief systems. Children deserve to be exposed to as many exciting ideas and thoughts as possible. And I hope that this play exposes them to one of the most extraordinary discoveries that we human beings have been lucky enough to inherit.

Characters

CHARLIE
A very angry nine year-old boy. Small

FITZ
Charlie's very strange looking dog. A cross between an Irish Wolfhound and a Beagle, with an unusual genetic mutation in the shape of a plum-pink bum that flashes like a Belisha beacon in the night. Tall

DAVID FATTENBOROUGH
A famous naturalist. Played by Charlie

CHARLES DARWIN
The greatest scientist the world has ever known ever. Played by Charlie

CAPTAIN FITZROY
The Captain of HMS Beagle. Played by Fitz

AN ADVERT
An American voice

A TALKING NEWSPAPER
A Cockney voice

The Ride of Your Life was first performed at Polka Theatre, London, 25 September 2009, with the following cast:

>CHARLIE, Michael Keane
>FITZ, Kyle Riley

>*Director* Mick Gordon
>*Designer* Naomi Wilkinson
>*Lighting Designer* Johanna Town
>*Sound Designer* Mike Furness
>*Choreographer* Sally Brooks
>*Assistant Director* Norifumi Hida

Act One

SCENE 1

On stage, an uncolourful orphanage with no furniture to hide behind. Suddenly from off stage, loud barking and yapping. CHARLIE's very strange looking dog, FITZ, has managed to sneak his way into the back of the auditorium. His barking and yapping become louder and louder until he bursts through the back doors. He sees the audience. Stops. Then smiles, chuckles and proceeds to cause general havoc: licking children, stealing handbags and of course farting. Eventually FITZ ends up on stage. FITZ's Irish side has caused him to have an overly-developed sentimental streak. And as soon as he is on stage he sings a sort-of Irish ballad, to the tune of Percy French's 'Come Back Paddy Reilly to Me'.

FITZ: (*Sings.*) Oh the Garden of Eden has vanished they say
But I know the lie of it still
Just turn to the left at the foot of Bencray
And stop when half way to Coot Hill
It's there I shall find it I know soon enough
Come whispering over to me
Come back handsome Fitz – (*Spoken.*) That's me name, *Fitz*.
(*Sings.*) Come back handsome *Fitz* to Bally James Duff
Come home handsome doggy to me…

Me beautiful big Irish Wolfhound of a Mammy used ti' sing that pretty wee song to me when I was but a pup of a doggy back in me greeny, green homeland of Ireland. And it was me Mammy that gave me the name Fitz. Because when I was born, I was so wee and small that she used ti' keep me in a shoe. And if the shoe fits Fitz, me Mammy used ti' say ti' me, then it's the name *Fitz* you should be given to wear. Do you want to see a photo of me beautiful big Irish Wolfhound of a Mammy? There she is. Isn't she a wonder to behold?

FITZ shows the audience a big photograph of his beautiful big Irish Wolfhound of a Mammy.

I loved me big Mammy, God bless her soul now departed and never to be seen again in anything solid or liquid or gas.

FITZ crosses himself quickly several times.

CHARLIE: (*Off.*) Ahhhhhh-Choo!

FITZ: Crikey O'Reilly! It's me master, Charlie! And he's got the flu.

CHARLIE: (*Off.*) Ahhhhhh-Choo!

FITZ: Coughs and sneezes, spread diseases.

CHARLIE: (*Off.*) Fitz! FITZ! Where are you? Come here you totally ugly creature!

FITZ: Hail Mary, Jesus and Joseph, did ye hear what me master Charlie's just after calling me? 'Totally ugly creature!'

CHARLIE: (*Off.*) Ahhhhhh-Chooo!

FITZ: Charlie's me master's name and it was the name given to him by the orphanage here. As well as me. They gave Charlie me to keep him company and make him feel not so alone, seeing how he was so cruelly abandoned as a baby and has got no family at all in all the world but himself.

CHARLIE: (*Off.*) Where are you Fitz, you totally *ugly* dog?

FITZ howls.

(*Off.*) And stop that howling you totally ugly and unnatural mutant!

FITZ: 'Totally ugly and unnatural mutant!' Did ye' all hear what me master Charlie's after calling me now?! And sure is it my fault that I'm a cross between two highly unsuitable breeds of doggy: Me beautiful big Irish Wolfhound of a Mammy and me mongrelly wee Daddy of an Beagle.

At the mention of the word 'Beagle' FITZ spits.

Okay. That's not the only reason me master thinks I'm a totally ugly and unnatural mutant. It's also because… because I've a strange and singularly inexplicable characteristic belonging to neither of me doggy parents in the shape of me plum-pink bum that flashes like a Belisha beacon in the night! Do you want to see it, me plum-pink bum? Well…if I be showing it to you, you have to promise me one thing. You won't laugh. You promise? Well okay then, here it is.

FITZ points his bum towards the audience and it immediately starts flashing like a Belisha beacon in the night.

You see. You couldn't help it could you. And that's what makes it all the worse. That me master Charlie's *right*. I am a totally ugly and unnatural mutant!

CHARLIE enters straight to the front of the stage. FITZ looks for something to hide behind. There isn't anything. So he stands particularly still and pretends to be a tree.

CHARLIE: (*To audience.*) Oi you lot! Yes you sitting right there! Have you seen my dog? Have you? Have you seen Fitz? Look. You can't miss him: long body, short legs and a plum-pink bum that flashes like a Belisha beacon in the night. A totally ugly and unnatural mutant. You have seen him. I know you have. Now where is he? He can't be hiding because there's nothing at all in the orphanage here to hide behind. Except for that tree. Ahhhhh-Choo!

The sneeze doubles CHARLIE over. Behind him we see FITZ.

FITZ: (*Bless you.*) Bless yapp.

CHARLIE freezes. And so does FITZ.

CHARLIE: Did that tree just bark a yappy bark at me? I thought it did! I must be going mad. Ahhhhhh-Choo!

CHARLIE sneezes again, this time all over his hands.

And now look! Coughs and sneezes really do spread diseases. Because now I've got greeny green snot all over my pearly white hands and I don't even have a hanky to wipe it off. Disgusting! And it's all my totally ugly and unnatural mutant dog Fitz's fault.

CHARLIE wipes his snotty hands on the tree then exits to get a hanky. FITZ stops pretending to be a tree and comes forward.

FITZ: No it isn't! It's not my fault me master Charlie's got the flu and it's not my fault that I'm so totally ugly. Me Mammy, God rest her non-gaseous soul, was a beautiful big Irish Wolfhound but her master took her to have a pup with me mongrelly wee Daddy of a Beagle. A right dodgy wee doggy if ever there was. See for yourself.

FITZ produces a photo of his Daddy.

That's him. Me mongrelly wee Daddy of a Beagle.

FITZ spits.

And what's worse he was an *English* Beagle! Can you fathom that? English! It still pains me paws to say it. But it was his elegant English bark what won me Mammy's heart and when me Daddy woof-woofed at me Mammy she was smit with love straight away and bing bang boom and Bob's your proverbial Uncle and sixty-three days later there was me.

FITZ's bum starts flashing again.

SCENE 2

On stage, a very big TV. On which DAVID FATTENBOROUGH, the world-famous naturalist, is about to explain evolution.

CHARLIE: There you are Fitz! Where have you been? David Fattenborough, the world-famous naturalist, is coming on television and I need to watch him even though I don't want to and I've got the flu even though I've had an anti-flu injection flu jab!

CHARLIE gets the remote control.

FITZ: (*To audience.*) Nature programmes. Fascinating and educational I admit, but what use are they to a totally ugly mutant dog?

FITZ snatches the remote control.

CHARLIE: Give me that back you totally ugly and unnatural mutant! David Fattenborough's going to explain evolution and I have to do my homework about it and I have to get a big Gold Star because if I don't get a big Gold Star I'm going to be expelled from school!

FITZ: (*Expelled?*) Bark Yapp?!

CHARLIE: Yes expelled. I got caught copying okay.

FITZ: (*To audience.*) Copying?! Crikey O'Reilly! But copying is illegal!

CHARLIE: (*During the following CHARLIE is trying not to cry.*) And it's not because I'm stupid! It's not! I'm not stupid! It's because it was Science. And I hate Science. I hate it so much I didn't even copy it right. I made a big MISTAKE. So the teachers found out. And copying is illegal! And now if I don't get a big Gold Star for my homework they're going to expel me! And it's going to be all your fault Fitz!

FITZ: (*My fault?*) Bark yapp?

CHARLIE: Yes Fitz, your fault! And no, I'm not crying. I'm not! Because people who cry are stupid. And I'm not stupid.

CHARLIE turns away to wipe his teary eyes. During this it becomes apparent that when FITZ talks all CHARLIE can hear is barking and yapping.

FITZ: (*To audience.*) He is crying. But he's not stupid. He just thinks he is. Full of self doubt is me master Charlie.

CHARLIE: Stop your barking and yapping I said!

FITZ: I will master. But honestly, I have to tell you, nature programmes are totally boring.

CHARLIE: (*Very angry.*) Look you mutant, I don't understand evolution, okay, and everybody else at school does, and if I don't get a Gold Star I'll be thrown out of school and everyone will laugh at me because I don't even have a family and I'll have to punch them all in their arms and give them dead-legs and tell them I don't care that I have no family when it's the only thing in all the world that I really do care about!

Beat.

Look Fitz. If I get you some tea will you sit quietly and watch the programme?

FITZ: And a bun.

CHARLIE: I don't understand you Fitz. But you know, sometimes, I get the feeling that you're trying to talk to me. And sometimes I wish I could understand you. Because then we could be proper friends.

FITZ: (*To audience.*) Proper friends?

CHARLIE: Stop barking I said! Look. If I give you a bun will you sit quietly and watch the programme?

FITZ: (*To audience.*) Sure isn't that what I'm just after sayin'? Honestly. Humans. They're awful silly things for the most clever animal on the Earth. They can't even copy Science homework without making a big mistake. And they can't even speak dog! (*To CHARLIE.*) Yes master Charlie. Bark, bark, yapp! If you give me a bun, bark bark bark, I'll sit as quietly as a quiety wee wood-mouse would, and watch the boring programme.

CHARLIE: I've just had it again. The feeling that you're trying to talk to me Fitz. I really am going mad!

THE RIDE OF YOUR LIFE: ACT ONE

Exit CHARLIE.

FITZ: Why does he want me to watch David Fattenborough the world-famous naturalist? I can understand that he doesn't want to get expelled from school, but what business do I have being educated? I, who never have any homework to do, being as I am, just a totally ugly mutant dog whose only dream is of being handsome?

DAVID FATTENBOROUGH now appears in the TV. He looks strangely like CHARLIE looks except that he is very, very fat.

DAVID FATTENBOROUGH: Good evening viewers. My name is David Fattenborough. And tonight I'm going to tell you all about evolution.

FITZ: Yawn!

DAVID FATTENBOROUGH: And about the greatest scientist the world has ever known ever, Charles Darwin.

FITZ: Even bigger YAWN!

DAVID FATTENBOROUGH: And his amazing voyage around the world with Sea Captain FitzRoy aboard the ship, HMS Beagle.

FITZ: Did he just say Beagle?

DAVID FATTENBOROUGH: Yes I did just say Beagle.

FITZ: Sure I thought that Beagle was indeed what you just did say.

DAVID FATTENBOROUGH: Well it was.

FITZ: Me Daddy was a Beagle.

FITZ spits.

DAVID FATTENBOROUGH: Was he indeed?

FITZ: A Beagle is indeed what me Daddy was.

DAVID FATTENBOROUGH: Then you should find this both fascinating and educational. Now, before Charles Darwin, when people were asked: Where do you come from?

FITZ: Ireland.

DAVID FATTENBOROUGH: No! I don't mean a place, I mean: Where do you come from originally?

FITZ: Originally?

DAVID FATTENBOROUGH: And before Charles Darwin when people were asked, most people said, from God.

FITZ: Hail Jesus, Joseph and Mary, and God bless me beautiful big Mammy's soul now departed!

FITZ crosses himself quickly several times.

DAVID FATTENBOROUGH: But one hundred and fifty years ago all that changed.

FITZ: It did?

DAVID FATTENBOROUGH: It did. Because that's when Charles Darwin wrote the most famous book in all of Science: *The Origin of Species.*

FITZ: The origin of what?

DAVID FATTENBOROUGH: Species.

FITZ: Bless you.

DAVID FATTENBOROUGH: Thank you.

FITZ: What's a Species?

DAVID FATTENBOROUGH: Groups of things like cats and fishes and humans.

FITZ: And dogs?

DAVID FATTENBOROUGH: Yes, and dogs.

FITZ: Crikey O'Reilly. So this book, *The Origin of…*

THE RIDE OF YOUR LIFE: ACT ONE

DAVID FATTENBOROUGH: *Species.*

FITZ: Bless you again. Everyone around here's catching Charlie's flu.

DAVID FATTENBOROUGH: Will you please stop interrupting me and let me get on with my television programme?

FITZ: Sorry Mr Fattenborough,

DAVID FATTENBOROUGH: That's okay. Where was I?

FITZ: Charles Darwin.

DAVID FATTENBOROUGH: Ah yes. That's right. One hundred and fifty years ago, Charles Darwin shocked the whole, entire world by explaining in his book *The Origin of Species*, that all of life on Earth came from the same one thing.

FITZ: You mean we all came from the same one beautiful big Irish Mammy?

DAVID FATTENBOROUGH: Well more like, we all came from the same one tiny little microbe.

DAVID FATTENBOROUGH holds up a tiny little microbe.

FITZ: Wow!

DAVID FATTENBOROUGH: Which lived in the mud when the Earth first began.

FITZ takes the microbe.

FITZ: Well hail Joseph and his wife and baby! Are you telling me that all of life came from this, including me?

DAVID FATTENBOROUGH: Yes. Absolutely every single living thing on Earth, including you, came from that tiny little microbe because of millions and millions and millions of years of evolution.

FITZ: You've lost me.

DAVID FATTENBOROUGH: You don't know what evolution means?

FITZ: Nope.

DAVID FATTENBOROUGH: Evolution means to change over time.

FITZ: No. Still don't get it.

DAVID FATTENBOROUGH: (*Taking back the microbe.*) Look. You don't look like a tiny little microbe do you?

FITZ: No. I look like a totally ugly and unnatural mutant dog called Fitz.

DAVID FATTENBOROUGH: Exactly. So this tiny little microbe changed over millions and millions and millions of years and produced…

FITZ: Me!

DAVID FATTENBOROUGH: Not just you Fitz. All of us.

FITZ: Crikey O'Reilly! So we *all* evolved from that tiny little microbe, including me? Including Charlie?

DAVID FATTENBOROUGH: Yes.

FITZ: So does that mean that I'm related to Charlie?

DAVID FATTENBOROUGH: It means that all of us are related to everybody! Now isn't that just amazing!

FITZ: That's just amazing!

DAVID FATTENBOROUGH: Amazing.

FITZ: Amazing is what that just is.

DAVID FATTENBOROUGH: That absolutely every single living creature, absolutely every single living *thing* is part of one very, very big family. Even yeast.

FITZ: Yeast?

DAVID FATTENBOROUGH: It's what they put in buns to make them big.

DAVID FATTENBOROUGH has a bite of a big yeasty bun.

FITZ: So if absolutely every single living creature and absolutely every single living thing is part of one very, very big family then that must mean that Charlie has a family after all! And it's me!

DAVID FATTENBOROUGH: Join me after the commercial break when I explain the rest of the entire history of life on earth.

Exit DAVID FATTENBOROUGH.

FITZ: Well I never did! Well I did once but it was a very long time ago and I still do regret it. Well, well, well. What do you make of that? We are *all* related. Wait 'till I tell me master Charlie! Charlie! Master Charlie come quick! It's amazing! It's a miracle in fact! And when you hear, you're going to be as happy as the happiest of happy things can be!

Enter CHARLIE with a big yeasty bun.

CHARLIE: I told you to stop barking and yapping and to be quiet! I even promised you a bun if you kept quiet. And look how big it is.

FITZ: That's because of the yeast.

CHARLIE: But here you are barking and yapping just as loud as you can. You are no replacement at all for a proper family at all!

FITZ: (*To audience.*) If only he could speak dog or if only I could speak human then he'd understand that he does have a proper family after all. And it's me!

CHARLIE: And now you've made me miss the first part of David Fattenborough! I hate you, you mutant! I hate you!

CHARLIE stuffs the bun in his mouth and eats it.

FITZ: My bun!

CHARLIE suddenly sneezes again and the stage and FITZ get covered in bun crumbs.

ADVERT: Welcome to THE RIDE OF YOUR LIFE! It whizzes, it whirls, it whooshes and WHAM: THE RIDE OF YOUR LIFE will whisk you so fast you'll travel back in time and get off before you got on.

CHARLIE & FITZ: Crikey O'Reilly!

CHARLIE and FITZ double take each other.

ADVERT: Crikey O'Reilly indeed! THE RIDE OF YOUR LIFE will be THE RIDE OF YOUR LIFE. Coming to the park near you TOMORROW!

CHARLIE & FITZ: TOMORROW!

ADVERT: Yes. TOMORROW!

FITZ: (*To audience.*) And it goes so fast, you'll get off before you got on?

ADVERT: It goes so fast it WILL SEND YOU BACK IN TIME!

CHARLIE & FITZ: WOW! IT WILL SEND US BACK IN TIME!

CHARLIE hugs FITZ with excitement. Then he suddenly realizes what he is doing and pushes FITZ away.

CHARLIE: And don't think I'm going to take you to The Ride of Your Life tomorrow Fitz. Because I'm not. Because tomorrow I'm going to the park by myself. Without you. Because you don't deserve to go on The Ride of Your Life. Because I hate you!

CHARLIE storms off.

FITZ: Please don't think too badly of me master Charlie. I know he shouldn't be illegally copying his Science homework. And I know he shouldn't be so horrible all the time. If only he could speak dog or I could speak human then I could tell him that he does have a family after all. A huge one. And that it's amazing because all of us are his family, including me. And then maybe he would stop doubting himself so much and stop all his crying and stop thinking that he's stupid and stop being so horrible and angry all the time and start having some fun and adventures with me! (*Change of tone.*) And another thing I was wanting to say. Or point out. Or mention in a sort-of questiony-like way is, do you not think that it's a wee bit weird that David Fattenborough looks so like Charlie, only older, and a lot fatter?

DAVID FATTENBOROUGH: That is a wee bit weird, but not as weird as the fact that four thousand five hundred million years ago…

FITZ: How many noughts is a million?

DAVID FATTENBOROUGH: Six.

FITZ: Six? I'm six.

DAVID FATTENBOROUGH: And the Earth is at least nine noughts.

FITZ: Nine? Charlie's nine.

DAVID FATTENBOROUGH: Nine noughts! The earth is at least nine noughts old.

FITZ: You mean the Earth is at least: Nought, nought, nought, nought, nought, nought, nought, nought, nought old?

DAVID FATTENBOROUGH: I do.

FITZ: Crikey O'Reilly, that is old!

DAVID FATTENBOROUGH: And when the Earth first formed, from the remains of an exploding star, everything was horribly hot.

An exploding star and fire. The fires get out of control. DAVID FATTENBOROUGH grabs a fire extinguisher. As he extinguishes the fires he continues.

But by a thousand million years later everything had cooled down. And the atmosphere smelt like a *gigantic* fart.

FITZ: David Fattenborough said fart!

DAVID FATTENBOROUGH: No I didn't.

FITZ: Yes you did. You said fart!

DAVID FATTENBOROUGH: No I didn't. I said, gigantic fart!

FITZ: He said it again!

DAVID FATTENBOROUGH: And this evil smelling chemical cocktail reacted with the water in the sea to form the tiny little microbe that I told you about that started all of life on earth.

FITZ: And to think I thought nature programmes were boring.

DAVID FATTENBOROUGH holds up a slithery wormy thing which he looks at through a big magnifying glass. The magnifying glass makes his eye go big.

DAVID FATTENBOROUGH: And after another thousand million years this tiny little microbe had changed, or?

FITZ: Evolved!

DAVID FATTENBOROUGH: Into a slithery wormy thing.

FITZ: Ugh! I hate worms. I've had them and they made me poo wormy poos.

DAVID FATTENBOROUGH: And after some more millions of years there were hundreds of different kinds of slithery wormy things and some of them evolved little by little into swimmy, squelchy things and some of them became fishes.

FITZ: Fishes!

DAVID FATTENBOROUGH produces a fish.

DAVID FATTENBOROUGH: Fishes.

FITZ: Ugh! I hate fishes. Not as much as I hate worms. But I hate them.

DAVID FATTENBOROUGH: And then after some more millions and millions of years some of these fishes evolved into nasty looking lizardy lizards. And then into bigger nasty looking lizardy lizards.

DAVID FATTENBOROUGH produces a nasty looking lizardy lizard.

And then into even bigger nasty looking lizardy lizards which were called?

FITZ: I know! I know! DINOSAURS!

DAVID FATTENBOROUGH: Dinosaurs! And some dinosaurs lived on the land and some dinosaurs took to the air in order to survive.

FITZ: In order to what?

DAVID FATTENBOROUGH: In order to survive! Look. If you were going to be eaten by a toothy big dinosaur what would you do?

FITZ: I'd run away.

DAVID FATTENBOROUGH: And if the toothy big dinosaur could run faster than you?

FITZ: I'd climb up a tree.

DAVID FATTENBOROUGH: And if the toothy big dinosaur knocked the tree over?

FITZ: Then I'd take to the air!

DAVID FATTENBOROUGH: And why?

FITZ: Because I'd want to survive! Now I get it! And did the Earth, you know, did the Earth still smell…pretty bad?

DAVID FATTENBOROUGH: Yes it did I'm afraid.

FITZ: Still like a gigantic fart?

DAVID FATTENBOROUGH: No, not as smelly as a gigantic fart. More like a really big dinosaury one.

FITZ: Keep going Mr Fattenborough. This is fascinating.

DAVID FATTENBOROUGH: And educational?

FITZ: Absolutely. If I could give you a big Gold Star I surely would.

DAVID FATTENBOROUGH: Well basically that's it. That's evolution. Over millions and millions and millions of years creatures changed in order to survive and eventually some of them changed into us.

FITZ: Crikey O'Reilly! But how do things change? How does evolution work?

DAVID FATTENBOROUGH now climbs through the TV to join FITZ.

DAVID FATTENBOROUGH: Well that's the million dollar question isn't it?

FITZ: If you say so Mr Fattenborough. But that's six noughts you're talking about.

DAVID FATTENBOROUGH: And it's the very question Charles Darwin answered in his amazing book.

FITZ: *The Origin of…*

DAVID FATTENBOROUGH: *Species.*

FITZ: Bless you. And what was Charles Darwin's answer to how evolution works?

DAVID FATTENBOROUGH: You're going to love this!

FITZ: Am I?

DAVID FATTENBOROUGH: Love it!

FITZ: Go on then.

DAVID FATTENBOROUGH: By bad copying and Natural Selection!

FITZ: (*Flat.*) By bad copying and Natural Selection?

DAVID FATTENBOROUGH: By bad copying and Natural Selection!

FITZ: You said I was going to love it Mr Fattenborough but I don't even know what you mean. And what's more, don't you know that copying is illegal?

DAVID FATTENBOROUGH: Only in school.

FITZ: What?

DAVID FATTENBOROUGH: Copying is not illegal in Nature. In fact, copying is what Nature does.

FITZ: Copying is what Nature does!

DAVID FATTENBOROUGH: Exactly. In Nature, microbes make copies of microbes, trees make copies of trees, humans make copies of humans…

FITZ: And dogs?

DAVID FATTENBOROUGH: Make copies of dogs.

FITZ: Crikey O'Reilly! So it was Nature that copied me beautiful big Mammy's body and me mongrelly wee Daddy's legs!

DAVID FATTENBOROUGH: That's right.

FITZ: But what about, you know… (*Pointing at his bum.*) How do you explain that?

DAVID FATTENBOROUGH: Bad copying. Because Nature always makes little mistakes when it copies.

FITZ: Little mistakes you say? I think you need glasses Mr Fattenborough! Just look at me bum! Just look at it! You call that a little mistake?

FITZ's bum starts flashing.

DAVID FATTENBOROUGH: No. I'd call that a big mistake.

FITZ: Well I'd call that a HUMUNGOUS mistake! Nature messed up its copying as bad as Charlie did when it copied me bum. So now I understand that Nature copies and sometimes humungously badly but I still don't understand the Natural Selection bit?

DAVID FATTENBOROUGH: Take it one word at a time. What does natural mean?

FITZ: It means Nature.

DAVID FATTENBOROUGH: Yes. Good. So Natural Selection?

FITZ: Well selection means choosing. So Natural Selection must mean Nature choosing.

DAVID FATTENBOROUGH: Exactly. Nature copies. It makes mistakes. Animals change. And then Nature selects which animals survive. And that, in a tough nutshell, is how evolution works.

FITZ: Well I never did, except for the time I mentioned before. But Mr Fattenborough, that's…that's so… How extremely stupid of me not to have thought of that.

DAVID FATTENBOROUGH: You're not the first to say so Fitz.

Exit DAVID FATTENBOROUGH through the TV.

FITZ: (*To audience.*) Now don't worry if you don't understand what Natural Selection means just yet. Because neither does me master Charlie. And when Charlie understands it, so will you. And that's a mutant doggy promise I'm making to each and every one of you, including you sitting right there.

Enter CHARLIE.

CHARLIE: Did I miss the programme? Yes I did! I missed it! This is all your fault Fitz for making me so angry!

FITZ: But you're always angry master Charlie. Being a little orphan boy who thinks he has no family at all in all the world but himself when the truth is master…

CHARLIE: Oh shut up and stop your barking and yapping. Now I'll never get a Gold Star because I still don't understand evolution!

FITZ: (*To audience.*) If only me master Charlie could speak dog or if only I could speak human then I could explain it to him.

CHARLIE: Bark bark yapp yapp, yapp yapp bark. I hate your barking. And I hate your yapping. But most of all Fitz, I hate you!

FITZ: Sure I know you do master Charlie, but just think, if both me parents had been beautiful big Irish Wolfhounds like me Mammy then I'd be an awful lot more handsome to look at. And maybe you wouldn't hate me after all.

CHARLIE: And now it's dark outside. And way past my bed time. And it's way past your bed-time too you totally ugly and unnatural mutant. So come on. Bed!

Exit CHARLIE.

FITZ: Hold on a minute. If I could go back in time and change me ugly mongrelly wee Beagle of a Daddy's evolution then I would change my evolution as well and then I'd evolve not to be such a totally ugly mutant doggy. And then my only dream in all the world of being HANDSOME would come true! And maybe I'd evolve to speak human! And then I could explain evolution to Charlie so that he could understand it like I mutant doggy promised. But how?

ADVERT: THE RIDE OF YOUR LIFE!

FITZ: It will whisk you so fast you'll travel back in time and get off before you got on!

ADVERT: THE RIDE OF YOUR LIFE WILL BE THE RIDE OF YOUR LIFE!

CHARLIE: (*Off.*) Fitz. Bed-time!

FITZ: Travel back in time! Of course! That's it! THE RIDE OF YOUR LIFE!

And with this FITZ jumps off the stage and disappears through the auditorium. At the same time CHARLIE runs back on stage.

CHARLIE: Fitz you totally ugly and unnatural good-for-nothing mutant dog. Where are you going? It's dark outside. And it's bed-time. Come back here! Come back! Don't leave me here in the orphanage on my own. Fitz! Now look! Now even my totally ugly and unnatural mutant dog hates me and he was the only thing that kept me from being so alone. I even got him a big yeasty bun for his tea and let him watch the television. And he knows I have no family at all in all the world but myself. And I'm not crying! I'm not! Because I never cry. Because people who cry are stupid. (*Shouting.*) And I don't care if you hate me Fitz! Because I hate you even more! And I don't care if I don't understand evolution. Because evolution is stupid. And I don't care if I get expelled from school. Because school is even more stupid than evolution. And I hate school. I hate it. It's a stupid place with stupid people where they teach you stupid things. Well it's all pointless and rubbish and I'm just fine on my own. And I don't need anybody else. Not family. Not school. Not you Fitz! Not anyone!

Exit CHARLIE.

Act Two

SCENE 1

A musical fanfare. On stage, a curtain of silver ribbons through which the newly evolved FITZ appears. He is now as handsome an Irish Wolfhound as ever there was, and he's dressed like Fred Astaire, complete with top hat, cane, tails, and a smart new collar. FITZ sings and dances to the following which goes to the tune of 'Putting on the Ritz'.

FITZ: (*Sings.*) Come and see the handsome new
    Dog who's on the avenue!
    All you people come and stare,
    At my nose up in the air!
    High hat and handsome collar,
    Lovely paws, I'm standing taller.
    What a handsome chum,
    And no more plum-pink bum!
    So if you're blue and you don't know,
    Where to go to, why don't you go,
    And change your bits?
    With the Handsome Fitz.
    Different now, evolved again,
    Beagle gone, a purer strain,
    With just me Mammy's bits!
    I'm the Handsome Fitz.
    Dressed up like a million dollar trouper,
    Changed my evolution now I'm super.
    Super-duper!
    Come, let's mix with handsome fellas,
    Walk with sticks, or umbrellas,
    In their mitts.
    I'm the Handsome Fitz.

Take the Ride and change your Life, no more ugly mutant strife,
I'll be such a hit!
The all-new Handsome Fitz!
AND… I can speak human! So now I can explain evolution to Charlie and he'll be as happy as the happiest of happy things can be!

CHARLIE: FITZ! WHAT HAVE YOU DONE!

Enter CHARLIE holding a duvet over his lower half.

FITZ: Hello master Charlie, the all-new Handsome Fitz at your service!

CHARLIE: Fitz. I can understand what you're saying. You can speak human!

FITZ: Isn't it wonderful master! Now we can be proper friends!

CHARLIE: And Fitz. You're so handsome.

FITZ: Who? Moi?

CHARLIE: Fitz.

FITZ: Yes master?

CHARLIE: (*Screams.*) I'm going to kill you!

FITZ: But why master, I thought you'd be as happy as the happiest of happy things can be?

CHARLIE: Because of this!

CHARLIE reveals his bottom half. He has turned into half boy, half fish.

FITZ: But master Charlie! You're half fish.

CHARLIE: I can see that you totally ugly and unnatural mutant who's suddenly become handsome.

FITZ: But I hate fish! Not as much as I hate worms but I hate them.

CHARLIE: How did this happen Fitz? What did you do? And why can you talk? And what are you wearing? I like the hat.

FITZ: Just a little trifle.

CHARLIE: Fitz! I'm half fish!

FITZ: Well look on the bright side master. I'm whole handsome with no more plum-pink bum that flashes like a Belisha beacon in the night. And the shock of the various transformations appears to have cured your flu!

CHARLIE: Ahhhhhhh-Choo!

FITZ: Well one out of two ain't bad.

CHARLIE: What did you do Fitz? Tell me the truth.

FITZ: Okay master. (*Fast.*) I went to the park to The Ride of Your Life and it whooshed and it whirled and I went back in time and changed my evolution so I could be as handsome as me Mammy wanted me to be and now you've got a fishy tail and your mouth is doing strange fishy movements that are making me feel like I've done something really, really bad and that I'm going to be in deeply serious trouble.

CHARLIE: You changed evolution!

FITZ: Only a bit.

CHARLIE: You went back in time?

FITZ: Only a little.

CHARLIE: FITZ!

FITZ: Soz.

CHARLIE: Soz!

FITZ: Yes. Soz.

CHARLIE: You've turned me into a fish Fitz and all you can say is 'Soz'?!

FITZ: Half a fish.

CHARLIE: I'm going to kill you!

FITZ: But master how was I to know that by fiddling with my evolution I'd be fiddling in turn with yours? David Fattenborough said we were all one big family and I wanted to explain… Oh dear, all one big family. So if I changed my evolution then I changed…

CHARLIE: My evolution as well! Fitz. We have to change it back!

FITZ: But then I won't be the handsomest of all the handsome dogs. And I won't be able to speak human anymore!

CHARLIE: I don't care Fitz!

FITZ: But it's what you wanted master, you said that sometimes you wished you could understand me so then we could be proper friends.

CHARLIE: I never said that.

FITZ: Yes you did!

CHARLIE: No I did not. Now, pick me up this instant and take me to The Ride of Your Life.

FITZ: But master…

CHARLIE: (*Trying not to cry.*) Now Fitz! We have to put this right or we're both going to be in even more trouble.

FITZ: You're right master, I feel it in me freshly reconstituted handsome bones. But please master, don't cry.

CHARLIE: I'm not crying! People who cry are stupid. And I'm not stupid Fitz.

FITZ: I know you're not, I was just saying…

CHARLIE: Don't call me stupid! Never, do you hear?! Or I promise you, I'll never ever ever be your friend.

FITZ: Sorry master.

CHARLIE: Right. Now take me to The Ride of Your Life. And get my torch. It's really dark out there.

FITZ: We don't need a torch master, I can use my plum-pink bum to help us survive!

FITZ looks at his bum.

Ooops.

CHARLIE: Come on Fitz. There's no time to lose.

FITZ picks CHARLIE up and they exit.

SCENE 2

Very dramatic music. Like Holst's 'The Planet Suite'. On stage, The Ride of Your Life. CHARLIE and FITZ enter. CHARLIE has a torch.

CHARLIE: Is this it?

FITZ: This is it.

CHARLIE: The Ride of Your Life?

FITZ: The Ride of Your Life.

CHARLIE: It doesn't look as good as it looked on TV.

FITZ: That's what I thought.

CHARLIE: Is it switched on?

FITZ: That's the strange part master. It's not.

CHARLIE: So how did it take you back in time?

FITZ: I just got on and thought about being handsome.

CHARLIE: What?

FITZ: That's what I did. I swear on me beautiful big Mammy's antediluvian soul!

FITZ crosses himself.

CHARLIE: Okay, I believe you.

FITZ: Right. So now what do we do?

CHARLIE: You have to have the same thoughts as you did before.

FITZ: Okay.

Beat.

CHARLIE: Nothing's happening.

FITZ: I can't remember what I was thinking. It must be the stress of the situation interfering with me brain.

CHARLIE: Come on Fitz. You have to. Were you thinking about your Mammy or your Daddy?

FITZ spits.

FITZ: Me Daddy. That ugly wee mongrel of a BEAGLEEEEEE…

The Ride of Your Life suddenly explodes into action, whizzing and whooshing CHARLIE and FITZ in all directions. Then BOOM! And they disappear.

SCENE 3

On stage, The Galapagos islands in 1835.

CHARLIE: Where are we? What happened? All you said was Beagle.

FITZ spits.

Why do you keep spitting?

FITZ: Don't know. Habit?

CHARLIE: Well stop it. It's disgusting. Ahhhhhh-Chooooo!

FITZ: And if I may say so master, so is that. And you know what coughs and sneezes spread.

FITZ gives CHARLIE a big hanky.

CHARLIE: Thank you. So where are we?

FITZ: No idea.

CHARLIE: You just said Beagle…

FITZ spits.

FITZ: Sorry master.

CHARLIE: And now we're here. But where is here?

A loud noise as the prow of the HMS Beagle appears.

CHARLIE & FITZ: Wow!

CHARLIE: I think you got the wrong Beagle Fitz.

FITZ spits.

FITZ: Sorry master. Maybe if you spell the word it would help.

CHARLIE: HMS B-e-a-g-l-e. That's a navy ship.

FITZ: And I've heard of it before. From David Fattenborough!

CHARLIE: What?

FITZ: Yes. That's it! It's the ship that the greatest scientist the world has ever known ever sailed around the world on with Captain FitzRoy.

CHARLIE: It is?

FITZ: It is.

CHARLIE: And who was the greatest scientist the world has ever known ever?

FITZ: Charles Darwin.

CHARLIE: Charles Darwin?

FITZ: He's the man who explained evolution.

CHARLIE: No way.

FITZ: Yes way. He even wrote a book about it. *The Origin of...* *The Origin of...* Something or other, can't remember.

CHARLIE: And that's his ship?

FITZ: That's his ship. The HMS B-e-a-g-l-e. What was that noise?

CHARLIE: Someone's coming. I think it's Charles Darwin and Captain FitzRoy! Quick, hide!

FITZ and CHARLIE hide as CHARLES DARWIN and CAPTAIN FITZ ROY enter.

CHARLES DARWIN: Captain FitzRoy?

CAPTAIN FITZ ROY: Aye Mr Darwin?

CHARLES DARWIN: Captain FitzRoy, we've been travelling together on the HMS B-e-a-g-l-e for over two years. So please, will you not call me Charles or even Charlie?

CAPTAIN FITZ ROY: I prefer Mr Darwin, Mr Darwin. What with familiarity breeding contempt and all.

CHARLES DARWIN: Very well Captain FitzRoy as you wish.

CAPTAIN FITZ ROY: Thank you Mr Darwin.

CHARLES DARWIN: Captain FitzRoy?

CAPTAIN FITZ ROY: Yes Mr Darwin?

CHARLES DARWIN: This is the fourth Galapagos island we've visited is it not?

CAPTAIN FITZ ROY: The fourth sir, aye.

CHARLES DARWIN: And all four islands are very close to each other, are they not?

THE RIDE OF YOUR LIFE: ACT TWO

CAPTAIN FITZ ROY: Like neighbours sir, aye.

CHARLES DARWIN: But why if they're so close to each other, why do the animals living on each island all look different?

CAPTAIN FITZ ROY: There are tortoises on all four islands sir.

CHARLES DARWIN: Yes, but their shells are all different depending on the island.

CAPTAIN FITZ ROY: A tortoise is a tortoise is a tortoise sir.

CHARLES DARWIN: That's easy to say Captain FitzRoy, but is it true?

CAPTAIN FITZ ROY: I'm sure I don't know sir. But then again, I *am* just a humble sea captain who likes his rum and the occasional shanty

CHARLES DARWIN: But it's like saying a dog is a dog is a dog. And there are many varieties of dog. Just like there are many varieties of human. But why are the tortoise shells different depending on which island we find them? Why is that?

CAPTAIN FITZ ROY: You ask a lot of questions Mr Darwin.

CHARLES DARWIN: I know I do, and I'm sorry Captain FitzRoy, but asking questions is what scientists do.

CAPTAIN FITZ ROY: I see sir. Well I must get back to the ship and see how lunch is coming along.

CHARLES DARWIN: Tortoise stew again Captain?

CAPTAIN FITZ ROY: No Mr Darwin. Today we're having a special treat.

CHARLES DARWIN: A special treat? Well that's wonderful Captain. Because to tell you the truth, I'm not sure I could eat another tortoise stew ever again in my life. So what's the special treat? What are we having for lunch today?

CAPTAIN FITZ ROY: Tortoise stew with nuts!

CHARLES DARWIN: Tortoise stew with nuts!

CAPTAIN FITZ ROY: Tough nuts. There are lots of them on this here island so I've put some in the tortoise stew to tasty it up a bit. It's going to be delicious. See you later Mr Darwin.

CHARLES DARWIN: See you later Captain FitzRoy.

Exit CAPTAIN FITZ ROY.

Tortoise stew with tough nuts. Disgusting!

The sound of birds. CHARLES DARWIN looks at them.

And the birds. What about the birds? On all four islands there are hundreds of little birds called finches. On every island. Except. Except their beaks are all different depending on the island. So on this Tough Nutty Island here, the finches have hard beaks and on that island over there which has no nuts, they have wiggly beaks. But why? And more importantly, how? How did that happen? Unless over time their beaks somehow changed depending on which island they were living on... Oh this is ridiculous! Will you just look at me! I'm talking to myself. I must be going mad. God created the world in seven days and seven nights six thousand years ago and then everything was washed away in a great flood except for Noah and two of every animal and that's all there is to it. All the same, if God didn't create every animal, if he didn't, and instead of being created all living creatures somehow changed, somehow *evolved...* (*Angelic sounds.*) No. Rubbish! I'm talking rubbish and what is more I'm talking it to myself! Thank goodness no one is here to hear me. I should go and eat some tortoise and tough nut stew and take my mind off my mind. But perhaps, just maybe, just maybe... I wonder. But how? How do animals change? How do they *evolve*?

Exit CHARLES DARWIN.

FITZ: Well as David Fattenborough would say, that's the million dollar question.

CHARLIE: Fitz, that was amazing! We saw Charles Darwin, the greatest scientist the world has ever known ever, in the flesh!

FITZ: And not only that Charlie, we saw Charles Darwin doubting himself! That's what's truly amazing. That even the most famous scientist in all the world ever had his moments of doubt. Just like you do sometimes master.

CHARLIE: Wow.

FITZ: Like we all do I suppose.

CHARLIE: Really? What, even you Fitz? Do you sometimes have moments of doubt, moments when you feel that no one in the whole entire planet understands you?

FITZ: I do master. Especially before, when I couldn't speak human and no one in the whole entire planet could understand me. But now I can speak human, so sit down and take the weight off your fishy tail and let me explain how evolution works. Evolution works by bad copying and Natural Selection.

CHARLIE: By bad copying! But copying is illegal Fitz! And I should know.

FITZ: Not for Nature master.

CHARLIE: It's not?

FITZ: Its not.

CHARLIE: And what's Natural Selection?

FITZ: It's all about survival master.

CHARLIE: It is?

FITZ: It is.

CHARLIE: So you really do understand how evolution works Fitz, and so you really can explain it to me?

FITZ: I really can master. But before I do, do you mind if I ask you something?

CHARLIE: You can ask me anything you like Fitz.

FITZ: Okay. Well. You know the way that you're called Charlie and I'm called Fitz.

CHARLIE: Yes.

FITZ: Well Charles Darwin is also called Charlie. And Captain FitzRoy is also called Fitz.

CHARLIE: Roy. He's called FitzRoy, Fitz. So what?

FITZ: Well do you not think that's a wee bit weird?

CHARLIE: How d'you mean?

FITZ: That they're called Charlie and Fitz and we're called Charlie and Fitz.

CHARLIE: It's just a strange coincidence Fitz. Hundreds of people in the world are called Charlie and hundr…

FITZ: Exactly. Fitz isn't so common a name now is it?

CHARLIE: I have to admit it Fitz. Fitz is not so common a name.

FITZ: Weird.

CHARLIE: Yeah. It is weird. Lets not think about it any more Fitz.

FITZ: Okay.

CHARLIE: Now explain Natural Selection.

FITZ notices a nasty looking lizardy lizard thing creeping towards CHARLIE.

FITZ: I will. But if I were you master Charlie I think I'd wait a wee bit longer before I do.

THE RIDE OF YOUR LIFE: ACT TWO

CHARLIE: No Fitz! I want to know. And I want to know now! Because if evolution works by bad copying and Natural Selection and I can understand it then I can get a big Gold Star in my homework and not be expelled from school!

FITZ: I understand that master, but I just think that at this very precise moment in time that there is something a tincy-wincy bit more urgent for you to be turning your half fishy attention to.

CHARLIE: What could possibly be more urgent than not getting expelled from school Fitz?

FITZ: A nasty looking lizardy lizard thing that's about to grab you by your wee fishy tail?

CHARLIE: A what?

FITZ: A that!

Now FITZ points at the nasty looking lizardy lizard thing that's about to grab CHARLIE by his fishy tail. CHARLIE looks. Then the nasty looking lizardy lizard thing grabs CHARLIE by the tail and begins to drag him off stage.

CHARLIE: Ahhhhhh! Help Me Fitz! A nasty looking lizardy lizard thing has got me by my fishy tail! Help me!

FITZ: I'm trying to master!

CHARLIE: FITZ!

FITZ: Got you.

CHARLIE: Now let's get back on The Ride of Your Life and let's get out of here!

FITZ: Right you are master! Let's goooooooooo!

They get back on The Ride of Your Life and off they go.

SCENE 4

On stage, the Age of the Dinosaurs.

CHARLIE: Where are we now?

FITZ: No idea. Crikey O'Reilly, what's that smell?

CHARLIE: Well what were you thinking when we got back on The Ride of Your Life?

FITZ: (*Extremely proud of himself.*) I was just thinking: Well thank the soul of me beautiful big Irish Wolfhound of a Mammy that the nasty looking lizardy lizard thing that was trying to nibble your wee fishy tail off wasn't as big as one of those toothy big dinosaurs that roamed the earth so many millions and millions and millions of years ago! That's all.

CHARLIE: You were thinking that when we got on The Ride of Your Life?

FITZ: I was.

CHARLIE: Oh Fitz.

FITZ: Hail Mary and her husband and son! What is that smell?! Master, did you just, you know, did you just do a gigantic fart? Well no, no, that's not fair, not a gigantic one, more like just a really big dinosaury one.

CHARLIE: No I did not! Anyway fish can't fart.

FITZ: Really? That must be why they have such funny looking faces. I mean if I couldn't let a wee fart slip out now and again me eyes would be as poppy-outy and anxious looking as a wee fishy's eyes tend to be.

Behind FITZ and CHARLIE the foot of a Tyrannosaurus Rex appears. CHARLIE sees it, FITZ does not.

CHARLIE: Fitz.

FITZ: And me mouth would be as tense and taught as a wee fishy's mouth. Due to all the stress I would be suffering what with not being able to do the gigantic fart that I needed to do.

CHARLIE: Fitz!

FITZ: Hold on a minute. Not gigantic, more like just a really big dinosaury one! Oh no master. David Fattenborough told me about when the world smelt like a really big dinosaury fart… Oh dear. Master Charlie, you're not going to like what I'm going to have to tell you. But I know where we are.

CHARLIE: And so do I Fitz!

FITZ: No you don't master.

CHARLIE: Yes I do!

FITZ: You don't!

CHARLIE: I do!

FITZ: You do?

CHARLIE: We're in the Age of the Dinosaurs!

FITZ: Well hail Jesus, and his Mammy and Daddy, I never did – except for the one time I told you about, but she was as beautiful a doggy as me beautiful big Irish Wolfhound of a Mammy was and so I just couldn't help me-self. Anyway, the Age of the Dinosaurs is exactly where we are! But how on earth did you know master?

CHARLIE: Because of that!

FITZ: Because of what?

CHARLIE: That!

Now CHARLIE points at the Tyrannosaurus Rex foot. FITZ looks.

FITZ: What? That giant dinosaury foot belonging to the Tyrannosaurus Rex, the most toothy and big of all the toothy big dinosaurs master?

CHARLIE: Exactly.

FITZ does a double-take.

FITZ/CHARLIE: CRIKEY O'REILLY!

FITZ: Run master! Or wiggle. Or do what ever half-boy, half-fishy things do!

CHARLIE: I'm trying Fitz!

FITZ: No wonder there are no half-boy, half-fishes in the world, they'd have never survived the dinosaurs.

CHARLIE grabs FITZ and holds him still.

CHARLIE: Shush! We're not going to out-run him so if we want to survive then we're going to have to be clever about this.

FITZ: You don't mean were going to have to use our intelligence master?

CHARLIE: That's exactly what I do mean Fitz.

FITZ: Then I think the intelligent thing to do would be to hide. But sure there's nothing at all here in the Age of the Dinosaurs to hide behind.

CHARLIE: Then there's only one thing for it Fitz. Were going to have to stand particularly still and pretend to be a tree.

FITZ: Pretend to be a what?

CHARLIE: If we both stand particularly still and pretend to be a tree then maybe the toothy big dinosaur will go away.

FITZ: That's the most ridiculous idea I have ever heard.

CHARLIE: JUST DO IT FITZ!

Immediately FITZ snaps into his tree pose which of course we recognise from Act One. CHARLIE does the same. The dinosaur lets out a very loud roar then slowly starts to go away.

FITZ: Well maybe a half-boy, half-fish would have survived after all, if he was as clever as you are Charlie what with the old tree pretending idea.

CHARLIE: You think I'm clever Fitz? Do you? Honestly?

FITZ: Honestly master, I do. So tell me this and tell me no more. Why are there no dinosaurs walking on the earth today? What happened to all the toothy big dinosaurs master?

CHARLIE: Well Fitz, you see that bright shiny light up there in the sky that looks like a playful little planet bringing joy and laughter to all the world below?

FITZ: Yes master I do. Isn't it lovely?

CHARLIE: Mm. Thing is Fitz. That bright shiny light up there in the sky is not lovely. What it is in fact Fitz is: DISASTER!

A dramatic sound.

FITZ: DISASTER?!

The same dramatic sound.

CHARLIE: Yes Fitz. DISASTER! Because that bright shiny light up there in the sky is in fact a deadly asteroid-comety thing plummeting towards the Earth, which will wreak havoc and destruction across the entire planet! Thus wiping out all the toothy big dinosaurs – and us – if we still happen to be here, all with one all almighty BOOM!

FITZ: With one almighty BOOM?

CHARLIE: Almightier than any BOOM you have hitherto imagined Fitz. So let's get out of here!

FITZ: Good thinking master.

They climb back on The Ride of Your Life as the asteroid-comety thing in the sky plummets closer and closer to the earth.

CHARLIE: Nothing's happening Fitz. Why's nothing happening?!

FITZ: It's because I'm scared master. And when I get scared I find it hard to think.

CHARLIE: But you have to think Fitz or The Ride of Your Life won't work.

FITZ: No. Can't. Too frightened.

CHARLIE: So what are we going to do?

FITZ: Well unless you can calm me down sufficiently to start my brain a-thinking what we'll probably do is die an extremely horrible comety death.

CHARLIE: Are you crying Fitz?

FITZ: (*Trying not to cry.*) No. People who cry are stupid. You said so yourself. And I'm like you master, I never cry!

CHARLIE: Okay, okay. So how can I calm you down?

FITZ: (*Suddenly smiling.*) Sing me a wee song like me Mammy used to do.

CHARLIE: We're about to die in one almighty BOOM and you want me to sing you a wee song?!

FITZ: It's my favourite thing in all the world.

CHARLIE: But I don't know any songs Fitz!

FITZ: Well I know lots so maybe if I sing one to you that will work just as well.

CHARLIE: Well come on then. Sing!

FITZ: I will if you dance.

CHARLIE: Dance?

FITZ: Just a bit.

CHARLIE: Fish can't dance Fitz.

FITZ: Oh now master, I think we both know that's not entirely true. Fish can groove on down with the best of them.

CHARLIE: Okay. Okay! Just start singing.

FITZ sings the following to the tune of Percy French's 'Phil The Fluters Ball'.

FITZ: (*Sings.*) Have you heard of handsome Fitzy
From the town of Ballymuck
Oh the times were going bad for him
In fact the dog was about to be mushed into a pulp by an asteroid
But he didn't care that much
Because he had a bestest friend
And though his friend was half a fish
That friendship will not end!

CHARLIE has stopped dancing but FITZ, now caught up in the song, has not yet noticed.

With a toot on the flute
And a twiddle on the fiddle-oh!
Hoppin' in the middle
Like a fishy on the griddle-oh…

You've stopped grooving master. Is something wrong – apart from our impending horrible comety death I mean? Is it because I sang 'Fishy on a griddle-oh'? Too close to the proverbial fishbone?

CHARLIE: Bestest friend Fitz? Did you just say that I'm your bestest friend?

FITZ: No. I definitely did not say that.

CHARLIE: You definitely did say that because I just heard you!

FITZ: I did not say it, I sang it. And that's a totally different thing.

CHARLIE: Why?

FITZ: Why master? Well I'm not entirely certain why. But when one sings, one's true feelings tend to issue forth without the constraints that polite society seems to demand of normal speech. I'm sorry master if my song made you angry. I really am.

CHARLIE: No you didn't make me angry Fitz.

FITZ: Yes I did master.

CHARLIE: No you didn't Fitz.

FITZ: I did. I know I did.

CHARLIE: (*Angry.*) No you didn't! Because that's the nicest thing that anyone has ever said to me! Ever! So now will you please think some thoughts and save our lives so we can enjoy our future together as bestest friends should.

FITZ: Well Crikey O'Reilly master, when you put it like that. Let's gooooooo…

Kerwhosh. And off they go.

SCENE 5

On stage, the future. It is very dark. In the distance hundreds of plum-pink lights flashing like Belisha beacons in the night.

CHARLIE: Where are we now?

FITZ: No. Still no idea. To tell you the truth I was just enjoying a wee thought about our future together as bestest friends.

CHARLIE: Our future together!

FITZ: As bestest friends.

CHARLIE: The future Fitz!

FITZ: Oh. Ooops.

CHARLIE: Ooops?

FITZ: Yes. Ooops.

THE RIDE OF YOUR LIFE: ACT TWO

CHARLIE: Oh Fitz!

FITZ: I suppose that's the end of the bestest friend thing?

CHARLIE: Well maybe the future's not that bad.

FITZ: Well master, it'll depend on global warming and whether or not we've managed to avert the Earth's impending energy crisis. Though I doubt it. Because next to big yeasty buns we all pretty much love those scrumptious wee ready meals and those delightfully frothy takeaway lattes don't we?

CHARLIE: What are you talking about Fitz?

FITZ: Absolutely no idea.

CHARLIE: Where is everyone? And why is it so dark? And what are all those plum-pink lights flashing like Belisha beacons in the night?

FITZ: You ask a lot of questions master, maybe you're going to be a scientist like Charles Darwin.

CHARLIE: Do you think I could be Fitz?

FITZ: I don't see why not. What's that?

A talking NEWSPAPER has blown onto stage. It is a cockney.

NEWSPAPER: I'm a talking newspaper.

CHARLIE/FITZ: A talking newspaper! Crikey O'Reilly!

NEWSPAPER: Crikey O'Reilly indeed.

FITZ: (*Aside to CHARLIE.*) What should we ask it?

CHARLIE: (*Aside to FITZ.*) We should ask it what the news is I suppose.

FITZ: Good thinking master.

CHARLIE/FITZ: What's the news newspaper?

NEWSPAPER: Listen all about it! Listen all about it! 'World Energy Crisis Averted! World Energy crisis Averted!'

CHARLIE: What does 'averted' mean Fitz?

NEWSPAPER: It means, stopped, stupid

CHARLIE: What did you just call me?!

FITZ: I'm sure the newspaper didn't mean it master.

NEWSPAPER: Mmm. I think you'll find I did.

FITZ: Ignore it Charlie. It must be a tabloid.

NEWSPAPER: What does averted mean? You are so stupid I bet you can't even copy your Science homework without making a big MISTAKE! And I bet that now you're going to cry!

CHARLIE: I never cry! Come here you…

CHARLIE is about to rip the newspaper into pieces.

FITZ: NO MASTER! NO! Please don't rip up the talking newspaper or we won't find out what the future has in store for us and that would be a terrible shame of a wasted opportunity missed.

Reluctantly, CHARLIE puts the newspaper down.

Thank you master.

CHARLIE: If he calls me stupid again Fitz, I'll shred him.

FITZ: That's fair enough. Now newspaper, as politely as you can, can you please tell us what the news is.

NEWSPAPER: 'World Energy Crisis Averted By Plum Pink Bum Mutant Dogs.'

FITZ: What did he just say?

NEWSPAPER: 'Mutant dogs with plum-pink bums that flash like Belisha beacons in the night have saved the world!'

FITZ: No way!

NEWSPAPER: Yes way! 'The Hero Dogs stand on every street corner when it's dark and guide people safely home at night and so save millions of pounds in energy that was previously used for street lights. So now the human race can survive and we can all continue to enjoy our scrumptious wee ready meals and delightfully frothy lattes.'

FITZ: Hero dogs?

CHARLIE: With plum-pink bums!

FITZ: That flash like Belisha beacons in the night and so save the entire world from its impending energy crisis?

CHARLIE: Plum-pink bums Fitz!

FITZ: Crikey O'Reilly! You mean like the plum-pink bum I used to have before I messed up all of evolution.

CHARLIE: Exactly.

FITZ: Well I never did!

NEWSPAPER: Well that's a porky-pie for a start. I think we all know that you absolutely definitely did mate!

FITZ: Only once! And only because she was as beautiful a doggy as me big Mammy was! But how did you know newspaper?

NEWSPAPER: Because it's your children's children's children's children with plum-pink bums that flash like Belisha beacons in the night that have saved the world stupid! And who do you think they got their flashing bums from originally?

FITZ: Well surely not from me?

NEWSPAPER: Yes stupid. From you!

FITZ: Crikey O'Reilly! Did you hear that master! The hero dogs that saved the world are my children's, children's, children's, children. And they got their plum pink bums from me!

CHARLIE: But Fitz, you don't have a plum-pink bum anymore.

FITZ: I never thought of that. Maybe it won't matter.

Suddenly the hundreds of plum-pink lights flashing like Belisha beacons in the night go out.

Ooops.

NEWSPAPER: News just in! News just in! Listen all about it! 'Evolution Changed! Plum Pink Bum Mutant Dogs No Longer Exist!'

CHARLIE: Oh no!

NEWSPAPER: Oh yes! 'World Energy Crisis Continues! World Energy Crisis Continues! Without Plum Pink Bum Mutant Dogs, the Entire Human Race will DIE!

CHARLIE: The entire human race will die! That's a bit dramatic isn't it?

NEWSPAPER: It's what sells papers mate. Listen all about it! 'Because of a strange and as yet unexplained change in evolution hero dogs that used to stand on every street corner when it was dark and guide people safely home at night with their plum-pink bums that flashed like Belisha beacons in the night no longer exist! And so the millions of pounds in energy that was previously used for street lights is no longer saved!'

CHARLIE: And so the world has run out of energy!

NEWSPAPER: 'And So The World Has Run Out Of Energy!'

CHARLIE: And so the entire human race will die!

NEWSPAPER: Oi mate. Stop stealing my headlines.

CHARLIE: Sorry.

NEWSPAPER: Yeah, right. Listen all about it! Listen all about it! 'Entire Human Race will DIE!'

CHARLIE: Oh Fitz. You have to get your plum-pink bum back! And this is much more important than me getting a big Gold Star for my homework. Because if we don't change evolution back to how it was then the entire human race will die!

FITZ: Well I never did.

NEWSPAPER: Don't start that again you stupid mutant! The whole world and his wife and his dog and his cat and his fish and his finch and his worm and his microbe knows you did!

FITZ: I told you already. Only once! And it was a very, very, very long time ago!

Whooooosh. And off they go.

SCENE 6

On stage, a very, very, very long time ago. Right back at the beginning where all of life began.

CHARLIE: Where are we now?

FITZ: This time I do know.

CHARLIE: You do?

FITZ: I do master. And so do you. Because it was the last thing I said to the talking newspaper.

CHARLIE: But you said, 'a very, very, very long time ago'! Oh Fitz, how long ago is that?

FITZ: Right back at the beginning where all of life began master. Nine noughts ago.

CHARLIE: I'm nine.

FITZ: Nine noughts!

CHARLIE: You don't mean: Nought, nought, nought, nought, nought, nought, nought, nought, nought ago do you?

FITZ: I'm afraid I do master.

CHARLIE: Crikey O'Reilly. Ahhhhhh-Chooo! Oh no! My flu's back!

FITZ: I wouldn't blow your nose if I were you master. I don't think you'll much like being right back at the beginning where all of life began if you can smell how it smells.

CHARLIE: Oh rubbish. It can't smell any worse than the Age of the Dinosaurs.

CHARLIE blows his nose.

Ugh WOW! That is worse. Much worse!

FITZ: I quite like it. It reminds me of Ireland somehow.

CHARLIE: I think I'm going to be sick.

FITZ: Better out than in.

FITZ produces DAVID FATTENBOROUGH's huge magnifying glass and CHARLIE's torch and starts looking for something.

CHARLIE: What are you looking for Fitz?

FITZ: Something David Fattenborough told me about.

CHARLIE sneezes and a large lump of luminous green snot comes out of his mouth and lands on the stage, directly under the huge magnifying glass.

FITZ: And there it is! Now do you see that tiny wee microbe in the mud?

CHARLIE: Yes.

FITZ: We'll that's all our Mammy. Or Daddy. Or both.

CHARLIE: It's what?

FITZ: That's where we come from originally. All of us. Including me. And including you, sitting right there.

CHARLIE: Don't be so stupid Fitz. How can we all come from that? I don't look anything like that. And neither does he, sitting right there.

FITZ: I'm not the one being STUPID master. You're the one being STUPID! The reason that you and I don't look like a tiny wee microbe in the mud is because of Nature's bad copying.

CHARLIE: What did you just say?

FITZ: Nothing.

CHARLIE: Yes you did Fitz. What did you just say?

FITZ: I said, 'Because of Nature's bad copying'.

CHARLIE: No Fitz. Before that. What did you say before that?

FITZ: I said, (*Mumbling.*) 'I'm not the one being STUPID master. You're the one being STUPID.'

CHARLIE: If you said what I think you said then I'll shred you and never ever be your friend again Fitz!

FITZ: I didn't.

CHARLIE: Are you sure?

FITZ crosses his paw fingers behind his back.

FITZ: Yes?

CHARLIE: Well good. So tell me again. How does evolution work and how do things change from that tiny little microbe into us? Ahhh-Chooo! And why do I still have my flu even though I've had an anti-flu injection flu jab?

FITZ: Well I don't know why you still have the flu master but I do know how evolution works. You should put your tail in the mud, your scales look a little on the dry side.

CHARLIE: Thanks. So go on Fitz. Explain.

FITZ: Well it's what David Fattenborough calls the million dollar question. How do different groups like humans and dogs evolve? And the answer is: By bad copying and Natural Selection.

CHARLIE: Well I know what bad copying is, don't I, but what does Natural Selection mean?

FITZ: Well take it one word at a time master. What does natural mean?

CHARLIE: It means Nature.

FITZ: Right. So Natural Selection? What do you think Natural Selection means?

CHARLIE: Well selection means choosing. So Natural Selection must mean Nature choosing.

FITZ: Exactly. Nature copies. It makes mistakes. Animals change. And then Nature selects which animals survive.

CHARLIE: Nature selects which animals survive?

FITZ: Yes. Think of Tough Nut Island and the little birds that Charles Darwin was talking about.

CHARLIE: The finches.

FITZ: That's them. Now the reason why there were only finches with hard beaks on Tough Nut Island was because only finches with hard beaks could eat the nuts. The other finches with wiggly beaks couldn't survive. Because their beaks were no good for eating nuts. And that's why it's called Natural Selection master. Because Nature selects which animals survive and which animals die out. And that's how evolution works.

CHARLIE: But I still don't understand Fitz. I just don't get it. I really, really don't. And I'm never going to get it! And I'm never going to understand. And I won't get a big Gold Star for my homework. And I'm going to be expelled!

And everyone will laugh at me and it's all because…it's all because…because… I AM STUPID FITZ. I AM STUPID!

FITZ: You're not stupid master, you're the cleverest boy I know!

CHARLIE: I'm stupid! I'm stupid! Stupid! Stupid! Stupid! I'm the most stupid boy in the whole entire world! I'm so stupid that I can't even copy my Science homework without making a big MISTAKE! And I'm so stupid that I don't even have a proper family!

FITZ: But that's not true master. I promise you. That's not true!

CHARLIE: What would you know?! You're just a totally ugly and unnatural mutant dog who messed up all of evolution and turned me into a fish! And you don't even have a plum-pink bum any more. I hate you!

FITZ is stunned and very, very upset. And so is CHARLIE.

I'm sorry Fitz. I didn't mean that. Any of it. I really didn't. It just came out. You're not unnatural. And you're not totally ugly. And you're not a *mutant*. And I don't hate you. Honestly I don't. You're my bestest friend in all the world ever.

FITZ: (*FITZ starts crying.*) No master, you're right. You're right. I am a mutant! And now look I'm crying! And you hate crying! So now you're going to hate me even more than you already do!

CHARLIE: Oh Fitz. I don't hate you. I really really don't.

FITZ: But I'm crying!

CHARLIE: And so am I.

FITZ: You are?

CHARLIE: Yes.

FITZ: But master, why are you crying?

CHARLIE: Because I still don't understand how evolution works.

FITZ: But master I think you understand more than you think you do.

CHARLIE: You do?

FITZ: Yes, I do. And I think you can even get a big Gold Star in your homework. But master. Tell me the truth. You really didn't mean it when you said that I was totally ugly?

CHARLIE: I really didn't Fitz.

FITZ: Even though Nature made a humungous mistake when it was copying me from me Mammy and Daddy and gave me a plum-pink mutant bum that flashed like a Belisha beacon in the night?

CHARLIE: Yeah. Especially because of that. Because…because I actually thought your bum was really cool Fitz. I thought it made you unique. You know, one of a kind. I was really proud of your bum Fitz. I should have told you that shouldn't I? And then maybe you wouldn't have caused all this mess by changing evolution and turning me into a fish.

FITZ: Half a fish.

CHARLIE: Half a fish. Sorry.

FITZ: Well I never did. Well once. But sure doesn't the whole entire planet know all about that now.

CHARLIE: And I don't think you're unnatural at all Fitz. I think you're very natural because your flashing bum helped you to survive in the dark.

FITZ: Well it did when I had a flashing bum.

CHARLIE: And that's Natural Selection! That's Natural Selection, isn't it Fitz?! And that's how evolution works!

FITZ: Is it?

CHARLIE: Yes. Nature copies. It makes mistakes. Like your bum. And if the mistake helps. Then the animal survives.

FITZ: Wow! And to think that it all started here is this slimy stinking cesspit.

CHARLIE: And if we ALL come from that tiny little microbe in the mud then does that mean…?

FITZ: It does indeed master.

CHARLIE: That all living things are related?

FITZ: You've hit the proverbial nail right on its poor wee bandaged head Charlie. We are all *related*.

CHARLIE: So I do have a family after all!

FITZ: Indeed you do master.

CHARLIE: Including you Fitz!

FITZ: Including ALL of us! Even him, sitting right there.

CHARLIE: Wow! I love you Fitz. I really, really, really do. You're the bestest family in all the entire world!

CHARLIE gives FITZ a big hug.

FITZ: Oh away with you, you silly wee half orphany half fishy master of mine, you have tears of joy bulging in me eyes and me throat as parched with emotion as a big humpy camel's dirty dry mouth would be if he was searching for water in a desert and having no luck finding a well.

CHARLIE: Come on Fitz. It's time to save the entire human race. And it's time for me to get a Gold Star in my homework. So come on, let's change evolution back to how it was before.

FITZ: But master…

CHARLIE: Fitz.

FITZ: But master if we change everything back to how it was before then I won't be able to talk to you anymore! And all you'll hear is my barking and yapping and then you'll hate me all over again.

CHARLIE: Oh Fitz. I won't hate you. You're my family. And from now on I promise to listen really hard to all your barking and yapping and I'll try to understand what you're saying.

FITZ: Is that a mutant doggy promise master?

CHARLIE: A mutant doggy promise is what that is. And just think. Maybe you, with your plum-pink bum are the origin of a totally new...

FITZ: Species!

CHARLIE: Bless you Fitz. I think you must be getting my flu.

FITZ: NO! That's the word. SPECIES! That's it! That's the title of Charles Darwin's famous book: *The Origin of SPECIES*!

CHARLIE: And that's what I have to explain in my homework!

FITZ: Yes!

CHARLIE: And you really think I can?

FITZ: Yes I do. So come on, time to go back to the unfishy Charlie and the old original Fitz – the origin of a totally new species!

CHARLIE: I'll say one thing Fitz.

FITZ: What's that Charlie?

CHARLIE: The Ride of Your Life has been The Ride of My Life!

FITZ: You're right there master. So let's get back on and let's get things back to normal! But before that, there's just one more thing I have to do.

CHARLIE: No Fitz.

FITZ: You'll thank me later.

CHARLIE: NOOOOOOOOOOOO!

Wher-whopperooo.

Act Three

SCENE 1

On stage, the orphanage from Act One but now very colourful indeed.

CHARLIE: I'm home. I never thought I'd be so happy to see the orphanage! And my fishy tail is gone! But where's my one of a kind unique dog Fitz! Fitz, where are you? Where are you Fitz!

From off hear loud barking and yapping from the auditorium.

Did you all hear what I just heard? Did you all hear that brilliant barking and amazing yapping?!

FITZ bounds on stage.

FITZ: Bark, bark, yapp, yapp, yapp!

CHARLIE: Fitz you're back! And? Let's see?

FITZ shows CHARLIE his bum. Beat. Then it suddenly shines like a Belisha beacon in the night.

You've got your plum-pink bum back! So the entire human race is saved!

FITZ howls a happy howl.

CHARLIE: But what was the one thing you had to do before you changed us back to normal Fitz?

FITZ: (*I'm scared.*) Bark, yapp.

CHARLIE: You're scared? But why Fitz?

FITZ: (*Because I think you're going to be angry with me.*) Yapp, yapp, bark yapp, yapp, yapp, yapp, yapp.

CHARLIE: Of course I won't be angry with you.

FITZ: (*You promise?*) Yapp yapp yapp?

CHARLIE: Of course I promise. I mutant doggy promise. But what did you do?

FITZ: (*I asked The Ride of Your Life to bring us back one day later than we left.*) Bark yapp yapp yapp yapp yapp,/ yapp yapp yapp yapp bark bark bark yapp.

CHARLIE: /You asked The Ride of your Life to bring us back one day later than we left!

FITZ: (*Yes.*) Yapp.

CHARLIE: But why?

FITZ: (*Ta da!*) Bark Yapp!

FITZ produces an enormous sheet of paper. It is CHARLIE's homework.

CHARLIE: What's that? It's my homework on evolution! And it's finished! Because it's one day later than we left – which means it's tomorrow already so I've already done it! Oh Fitz, you're a genius!

FITZ: (*Well, go on...*) Yapp, bark bark...

CHARLIE: What? Read it out in front of everybody?

FITZ: (*Yes.*) Bark.

CHARLIE: Well. Okay then. I'll do it for you

CHARLIE clears his throat. Reading out his homework in front of everybody is his final hurdle.

'How my Bad Copying and my Naturally Selected Dog Fitz taught me all about evolution.' Look Fitz! You're in the title!

FITZ howls another happy howl.

CHARLIE: 'The most utterly amazing fact of life is that we are all – all of us – one very, very big family. And that absolutely every single living thing on earth comes from the same one tiny little microbe in the mud including me, and including you sitting right there. Fitz.

FITZ: Woof!

CHARLIE: 'And over millions and millions and millions of years this tiny little microbe had lots of baby microbes. And some of the baby microbes were slightly different from their parents because like me, Nature is bad at copying.

FITZ: (*That's right!*) Bark yapp!

CHARLIE: 'And so life on planet Earth began to change. And through millions and millions and millions of years of little changes and bad copying different SPECIES emerged. Like fishes and lizards and dinosaurs…and monkeys and humans…and of course, dogs!

FITZ lets out an even happier howl than before.

And this process is known as evolution. Evolution means to change over time and it was explained by the greatest scientist the world has ever known ever, CHARLES DARWIN! Evolution explains why there are so many species on the Earth, and why there are so many varieties of birds like finches.

FITZ: (*And dogs!*) Bark bark!

CHARLIE: And varieties of dogs like my dog Fitz. 'So how does evolution work? It's what the world-famous naturalist David Fattenborough calls the million dollar question: And the answer is:

FITZ: /Bark yapp bark bark bark, bark yapp bark bark bark!

CHARLIE: /'By bad copying and Natural Selection!'

CHARLIE: 'Bad copying and Natural Selection is how evolution works. And the best way to understand it is, to think of my dog Fitz.' Look Fitz, you're my example!

FITZ: (*I am?*) Bark yapp?

CHARLIE: Yes! Yes Fitz, you are!

FITZ: (*To audience.*) Well hail Jesus and his Mammy and Daddy and his brother and sister and aunt! I've never been any one's example before in all me life!

CHARLIE: Sit down Fitz. The next bit is all about you. 'My dog is a cross between two types of dog: an Irish Wolfhound and an English B-e-a-g-l-e. And as you can see from these photographs (*CHARLIE shows us the photographs of FITZ's Mammmy and Daddy.*) Nature has copied characteristics from both his parents. Like his beautiful big body from his Mammy and his mongrelly wee legs from his Daddy. Because in Nature all animals, including you and including me, get characteristics from their parents. And some of these characteristics can help us to survive. Like if you're a finch on a tough nut island. If you have a hard beak that's good for eating tough nuts, then you will survive, and if you don't, then you won't. And this is called Natural Selection. Because Nature selects what survives and what doesn't. And animals that survive have children of their own, and Nature copies the parents. But sometimes Nature is very *bad* at copying, and once again my dog Fitz is my example. My dog Fitz has got one unique characteristic, all of his very own that he didn't get from either of his parents. His beautiful plum-pink bum that flashes like a Belisha beacon in the night!

FITZ sticks his bum out at the audience and it immediately starts flashing.

And this is called a *mutation*. And he got this mutation because sometimes Nature is as bad at copying as I am. And if this mutation helps him to survive then Nature will give it to his puppy children and they will all have plum-pink bums too. And if this happens then my dog Fitz will be the origin of a totally new species!'

FITZ: (*To audience.*) I bet you he didn't tell them about me and my children's children's children's children solving the world's impending energy crisis and saving the whole entire human race!

CHARLIE: (*Aside to FITZ.*) I didn't tell them about you and your children's children's children's children solving the world's impending energy crisis and saving the whole entire human race. I just didn't think they'd believe me.

FITZ: (*To audience.*) Honestly. Humans. They're awful silly things for the most clever animal on the Earth. They can't copy Science homework without making a big mistake. They can't solve their own impending energy crisis. And they can't even speak dog!

CHARLIE: 'And that's why Charles Darwin called this process Natural Selection. Because Nature selects the characteristics that help species survive. Like beaks on finches or cleverness in humans or plum-pink bums on dogs. And that's how evolution works. By Natural Selection. And that's how new species like my dog Fitz evolve. Because of mutations. Because like me, Nature is bad at copying.' Fitz?

FITZ: (*Yes?*) Bark?

CHARLIE: Guess what I got for my homework?

FITZ: (*I don't know.*) Bark, yapp bark.

CHARLIE: Oh Fitz…

CHARLIE pretends to be disappointed then shouts at the top of his voice.

I got A BIG GOLD STAR! /CRIKEY O'REILLY!

FITZ: /CRIKEY O'REILLY!

CHARLIE: You know what this calls for cousin? Your favourite thing!

FITZ: (*A bun?*) Yapp yapp?

CHARLIE: No. Not a bun silly. Much better than that. Your most favourite thing in all the world.

FITZ: (*To audience.*) He doesn't mean a wee song and a wee dance does he?

CHARLIE: That's exactly what I do mean Fitz! A wee song and a wee dance!

FITZ: (*To audience.*) Well CRIKEY O'REILLY INDEED!

FITZ howls once again. Music. Then CHARLIE sings and FITZ barks and yapps and sometimes sings the following 'Putting on the Fitz' reprise.

CHARLIE & FITZ: Come and see the handsome new
Dog who's on the avenue!
All you people come and stare,
At my nose up in the air!
High hat and handsome collar,
Lovely paws, I'm standing taller.
What a handsome chum,
With his lovely plum-pink bum!
So if you're blue and you don' know,
Where to go to, why don't you go,
And change your bits?
With the Handsome Fitz.
Bestest friends, evolved again,
All related, in Life's game,
With all me mutant bits?
I'm the Handsome Fitz.
Dressed up like we're million dollar troupers,
We are all changed back and now we're super.
Super-duper!
Come, let's mix with handsome fellas,
Walk with sticks, or umbrellas,
In their mitts.
Charlie and the Handsome Fitz.
Dressed up like we're million dollar troupers,
We are all changed back and now we're super.

Super-duper!
Come, let's mix with handsome fellas,
Walk with sticks, or umbrellas,
In their mitts.
CHARLIE AND THE HANDSOME FITZ…!!!

They both bow.

End of Play.